V I L L A

HOME SPACE AND
INTERIOR DECORATION

DESIGN MEDIA PUBLISHING (UK) LIMITED

CONTENTS

Haitang Villa

▶ Neo-Chinese Style

Designers
HAN Wenqiang & LI Yuntao
(Arch Studio)

Photographer
Magic Penny (www.
zoomarch.com)

Area
510m²

Materials
latex paint/oak veneer/
marble/stainless steel

Location
Beijing, China

Located in a residential area of Beijing east suburb, it is one of the three-floor town villas. The ground floor and the basement are thoroughly connected for catering visitors; the second floor has independent entrance and exit.

To be in harmony with nature has long been an ideal pursued by the Chinese people. Then how to present such an ideal under contemporary residence conditions? The key is that the villa is designed on the principle of "relationship" rather than "form", after taking the interactions between the interior and the exterior with the reference of traditional Chinese architecture design experience.

1. Semi-transparent walls substitute the normal sealed partition, which enforces horizontal levels and flows, allowing the expansion of outdoor light and scenery to indoors.

2. The underground courtyard is not glass-roof covered, a way commonly adopted in communities; instead it is treated as an integral part of the interior and is transformed into an area of bamboos and pebbles, connecting atmospheres of the interior and the exterior.

3. The natural materials, invisible lighting and furniture accessories of the interior design integrate with the overall space to create a plain and tranquil residence atmosphere with oriental flavor. The primary concept of design is to obscure the original relationship between the interior and the exterior by using the changes of materials and space; thus it creates an open and multi-faceted wandering environment, which frees the interior from local decoration and helps it return to a natural, plain, and tranquil residence atmosphere .

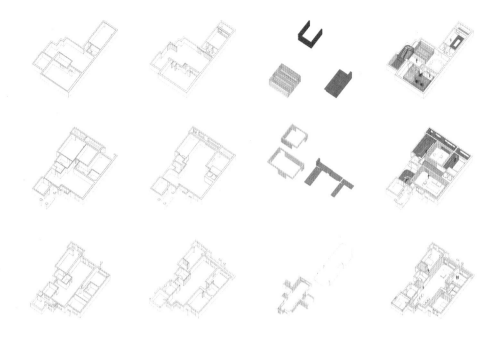

Diagram

First floor plan

Ground floor plan

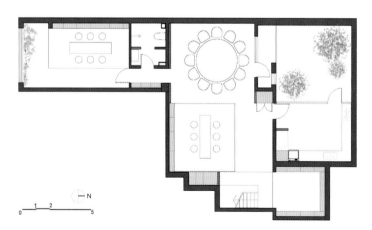

Basement plan

Decoration and Furnishing

The ground floor unfolds around the sitting room and study, in which the oak grid and shelves are used for book storage, exhibition and display. Simultaneously, semi-transparent levels are distributed from outdoors to indoors. The tea room uses cement paint in combination with customized table tops made in concrete. The contrast between the gray box and its background forms a variety of spatial feelings, which is true of the sitting room. The basement floor reallocates the courtyard and the inner space, and the bamboos planted in the courtyard make the basement interact with the outdoor landscape. The garage on this floor is transformed into a bright guestroom. A dome is implanted on the first floor, which makes the roof and walls integral with variations.

Invisible lighting is preferable in the design to avoid dazzle. LED linear lights are used on the ground floor to render the space tender and bright. As decorative lighting, floor lamp, ceiling lamp and some wall pictures are highlighted by spot lighting (3500-4000k). In contrast, spot lighting is minimized on the ceiling. Light belts are commonly used underground and LED spot lighting is hidden among bamboo groves. A number of LED down lights are arranged on the first floor, rendering starry effect.

The design is nature-oriented and doesn't adopt man-made landscapes. The entire courtyard is embraced by vertical wooden grids, forming an entire wooden background. White pebbles are used on the ground paving where sewage outlets are underneath. Bamboo groves, with several boulders as ornaments, and wooden grids set off each other. At the center of the courtyard is an iron-welded table, catering for tea chat when the weather is agreeable.

Furniture Design and Materials

The furniture and the space adopt integrated design. The furniture on the ground floor and the basement floor are mainly wooden. Couch and table are traditional Chinese flavored. White sofa and ink carpet on the first floor are well matched with the sitting room.

Materials are natural, plain and amiable at their utmost.
Ceiling: latex paint/oak veneer/cement paint/ mirror finished with stainless steel

Walls: latex paint/oak veneer/oak grid/cement paint/white marble/printing glass

Ground: white epoxy self-leveling/glued pebbles/gray self-leveling/white marble/wood grain brick

Correlations of selected materials are limited within three colors: white, gray and wood. And they are well matched.

Sea Pearl
Villa

▶ Neo-Chinese Style

From the cultural origin, LSDCASA team traces the design principle in the project of Sea Pearl Villa. Aesthetics of the Song dynasty, shokunin kishitsu, and research on the Chinese daily life are the prerequisites of the design.

The appeal of the "Unity of Man and Nature" is integrated into modern life concept. Apart from the maintenance of the soul of traditional Chinese style, the design exhibits modern, simple and elegant space, making a perfect realization of liveliness and peace both environmentally and spiritually, and generating more possible associations.

The core of the design is to cut through complexity and to exhale the old and inhale the new. Thus, the design gives up the superficial pursuit of styles or manners; instead, it seeks for available approaches of connection, communication and coordination in aspects of emotion, culture, temperament and recognition, and by means of this the design expresses a spiritual appeal.

Designer
GE Yaxi (LSDCASA)

Photographer
LSDCASA

Area
270m^2

Materials
marble/cotton and linen/
solid wood

Location
Shanghai, China

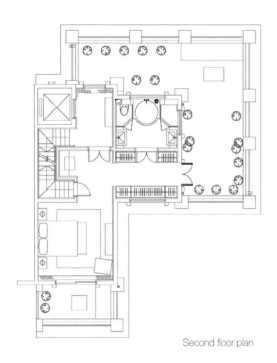

Second floor plan

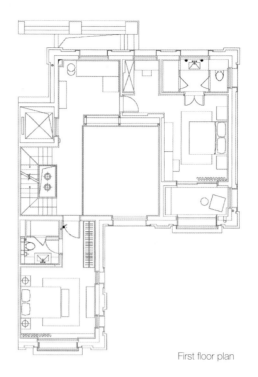

First floor plan

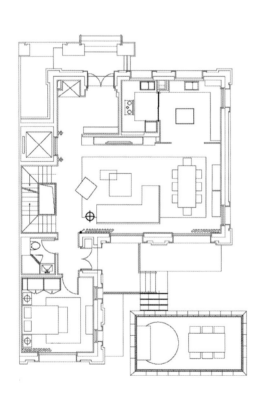

Ground floor plan

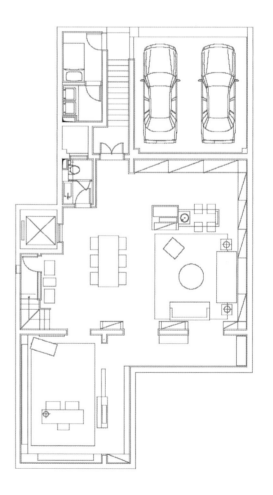

Basement plan

Decoration and Furnishing

The sitting room and the dining hall are both simply designed. The modeling and texture of drop lights correspond with the background in the space. The lead white color peaches on black porcelains are apparently elegant and the painting of the autumn declares magnificence of landscape .

In collocation with space, most articles are matte glazed or ceramic wares. Correspondingly,

ceramic or painted utensils are the presentation of traditional Chinese palace furniture and traditional Japanese paintings. Embellishments of bronze antiques of the Shang and the Xia dynasties add historical scent to the space. Besides, the introduction of traditional floriculture extends endless prospect in space, and flower arranging attaches importance to tempo and rhythm, which interprets the culture spirit of space.

Direct and concise lines, free and relaxed manner are the best interpretations of space. The cotton and linen materials are soft and comfortable. The weaved tea table sends forth intricate interest of Oriental impressions. Only a few added copper color embellishments not only make the space plain and elegant, but also extract contemporary temperament appropriately compatible with space.

Color Matching

Rooms and the study are connected at the basement, where the tone of space features blue, dark green and gray apart from burly wood. These colors derived from nature are implicitly expressed and bring freshness to the view at the same time. The private bedroom follows peace and elegance of the entire space and reminds us of the past, the present and the future and the evolution and mixture of Oriental humanities among colors and within certain forms.

Waterfront Villa

▶ Neo-Chinese Style

Designers
HUANG Shuheng & LIN Yinwen (Sherwood Design)

Decoration
WU Jialing, ZHANG Hedi, SHEN Ying

Photographer
WANG Jishou

Area
357m² (including courtyard)

Materials
alveolar stone/white marbles/Srp./gold leaf/dyed veneer/acid pickling mirror/PVD/wenge wood

Location
Suzhou, China

Suzhou, an ancient waterside town like Venice in Italy, boasts unparalleled waterside scenery and exquisite culture. While it reminds people of endless memories by gentle breeze, graceful pillows, weeping poplars and slight touch of the city, the modern landscape built at the historical site makes it possible to have a dialogue between the present and the past. The overlap of time and the intersection of space lay the foundation of Waterfront Villa.

Adhering to *The Travel of Marc Polo*, Sherwood Design tactfully transformed the confrontation between Western explorers and Oriental khan into a mix of Chinese and Western styles. The graceful aroma, exclusive to Suzhou, finds good expression in modern textures and traditional lines.

First floor plan

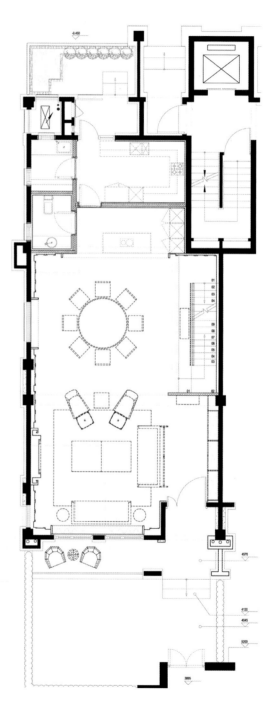

Ground floor plan

Furniture Design and Materials

The complicated paper-cut decoration of renowned architect Frank Lloyd Wright (1867-1959) comes into view on entering the hallway. The sleek decorative lines correspond with the opposite flower patterns made of gold leaf, exhibiting dramatic tension of oriental and Western elements. Several golden window grills are embedded into the wall as traditional ornaments and an instrument to enrich visual effects. Furthermore, Sir HUANG Shuheng changes the space scale by the reflection of stainless steel mirror ceiling to reinforce its magnificence. The division between the sitting room and the dining hall is clearly outlined by the air outlets connected with the indented ceiling, and it reinforces visual effects and displays the magnificence of the mansion.

Color Matching

Sherwood Design uses the basic color of lake green and integrates traditional elements (e.g. sofas with copper coin grains) with modern craft closely. By the change of proportions and the imitation of bamboo texture, the color matching presents traditional Oriental flavor. While the wall panels on the second floor are Chinese style in proportion, fancies are hidden on both sides. The mix of Chinese and Western styles are presented in a set of color variations.

Origin Villa

- To Infuse Innovative Oriental Flavor into Modern Metropolis Space

▶ Neo-Chinese Style

Design Company
LI Yizhong Space

Photographer
LI Yizhong Space

Area
500m²

Materials
Eurasian wood grain
marble/wood flooring/
blue enchantress marble/
leather/wood veneer/
wallpaper/hard-pack/wire
glass

Location
Dongguan, China

Located beside the Fifth Ring Road (opposite to Yingbin Park) in Nancheng district, Dongguan city, Origin Villa is alongside Dongguan Botanical Garden and enjoys distinctive geographical environment, boasting the only green landscape resource, at the city centerl. The villa is built according to the standard of South China high-end landscape luxury residence, and furthermore it upgrades the standard.

In view of resource maximization, humanity design, core space, construction and surrounding landscape and transition space between the interior and the exterior, the designer analyzed the housing type and created a four-floor luxury residence with emphasis on taste and manifestation of high quality.

Applying modern design approaches, the designer manipulates neat and clean hues on the basis of simple but sophisticated concept to achieve simple unity in form. Meanwhile, the designer lays emphasis on coziness and highlights the sense of design with exploration of absorption and innovation of oriental elements so as to create a modern metropolis space in combination with oriental culture.

Second floor plan

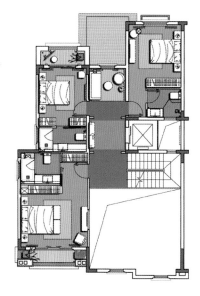

First floor plan

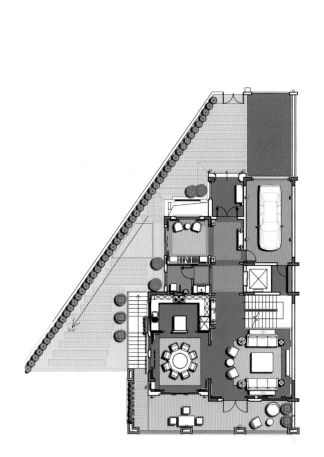

Ground floor plan

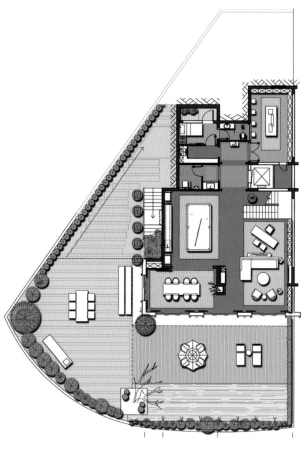

Basement plan

Furniture Design and Materials

In the designer's eyes, a house is likened to a skeleton, and in consequence, the design must be tailored for the construction structure. As different people have a range of clothing styles, different spaces must have distinct appearance compatible with their own style. Thus, the villa is labeled as a landscape residence filled with Oriental flavor.

At the early stage of the design, housing type and space utilization were taken into account. The basement level is comparatively independent and leisurely. Thus, this floor is designed for family union, calligraphy and painting practice, lounge, snooker, tea art, collection, washroom, staff and storage in separate sections.

The ground floor is designed for porch, hallway, garage, side hall, washroom, living room, dining hall, kitchen, passage, balcony and courtyard. The first floor is for parents suite, boy suite, girl suite, small living room and balcony. The second floor is for host suite, entertainment balcony, study and passage. The designer integrated balcony into the host suite, enlarging the landscape area, and adding life interests.

Color Matching

The overall space features creamy white and blue diamonds, together with shining colors like orange added in some accessories. The hues are clean and neat, conforming to the simple design concept.

Pearl River City Block
A5 G10-02 Unit Villa

▶ Neo-Chinese Style

Quietly located in the north of Conghua, Guangzhou, the Liuxi River glitters in the sunshine and is immersed in green shades all year long. Though it lacks prosperity and variety as the Pearl River, it boasts unique pleasantness and interest free from the bustling city. Near the Liuxi River, the Villa possesses geographic advantage. As a super-city complex worth 38 billion RMB invested by Pearl River real estate, the project of Pearl River City has a total planning area of nearly 1,270 hectares.

The designers integrated Oriental aesthetics with modern lifestyle to create an artistic atmosphere, and they also tried to infuse vibrant colors and modern aesthetics into the human-quality based Chinese simplicity style to get good command of every living detail and present beauty in co-existence.

The interior space retains the original sitting room of nearly 7 meters high, not only impressive but also complementary by partitions connecting two layers of space tactfully.

Designers
PENG Zheng, XIE Zekun, WU Jia (C&C Design)

Photographer
C&C Design

Area
410m²

Materials
marble/rose gold/glass/
leather/wood veneer/
wallpaper

Location
Conghua, Guangzhou, China

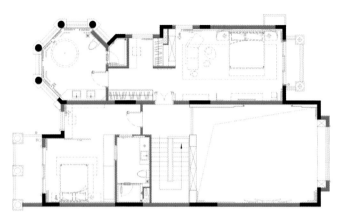

First floor plan

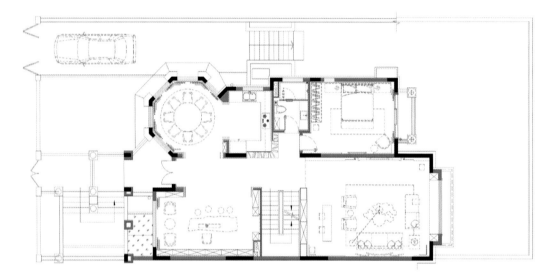

Ground floor plan

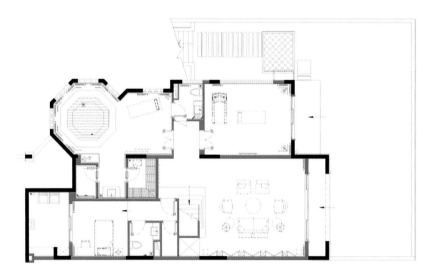

Basement plan

Furniture Design and Materials

The location of tea room in the dining hall adheres to conventions and connects with contemporary aesthetic creations. The open kitchen, together with the tea room forms a scene in front of us—as the wife and her friends are exchanging cooking experience, the husband is chatting with his friends over the tea, and kids are playing delightfully in the garden. Thus, trinity or unity is achieved in either

expressive force of space or appealing force of life.

The room for the seniors is on the ground floor for their convenience; nanny room is equipped with independent bathroom and connects the workshop. Such humanity design impresses us as if we felt the joyful atmosphere of the family. Through the transition of handrail made of

transparent glass, and embellishment of linear approach on the wooden veneer, we, with one-step-one-scene interest, step into the basement 1 where the wine area and the fitness room are located. Shades of sunlight are shed into the outdoor garden. The large SPA area is equipped with bubble bath and sauna with pasted agates, as luxury as they are.

Aquatic Villa

▶ Neo-Chinese Style

During the period of Yong Le in the Ming dynasty, Zheng He's expedition to the West opened the "maritime Silk Road", and since then exotic cultures began to spread in China. Till now, people are still fascinated by the Buddhist charm underlying the Southeast Asian culture.

Inspired by the "maritime Silk Road", KKD adopts typical Southeast Asian culture in the design of Aquatic Villa with delicate taste; thus it forms an ecological and romantic home space and creates a way of life that people return to plainness and quietness from showiness and bustling.

In reality, the interior design is a design for life. Since people living in tropical region admire nature most, Kenneth Ko lays emphasis on tropical flavors. For example, the narrow alley. It is transformed into an avenue paved with black cobbles and white marble slabs with tropical woods lined on both sides. Thus, a sense of nature and romance can be felt as we are wandering on the avenue.

Designer
Kenneth Ko (KKD Design
Co, Ltd.)

Photographer
KKD Marketing Department

Area
800m^2

Materials
black cobbles/white marble
slab/rosewood/carved wood

Location

First floor plan

Ground floor plan

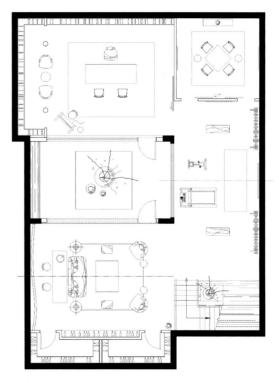

Basement plan

Decoration and Furnishing

Open the gate, and you will notice the emergence of the primitive and sensuous Southeast Asian culture in the seemingly careless layout of Buddha's head, wooden carving, pot, woven carpet, etc.

The Southeast styled home space is filled with leisure holiday flavor. Collaborated with proper decoration, the refreshing and comfortable atmosphere created by the furniture in simple lines and plain colors gives a full display of sacred and sensuous features of Thai culture.

Every decoration detail, from lotus-shaped drop light to carved wood furniture, is well worth appreciation.

In the design of the senior room, KKD employs brilliant daylight and well-designed lighting to create beautiful light and shadow. The antique flower-carving bed frames, collaborated with gold color woven carpet, exhibit dignity underlying calmness.

Fresh and graceful qualities of the guest bedroom are displayed by pea green wall-paper texture carpet, lotus leaf pattern quilt and the ornaments of Thai fabrics and copper art walls. Wooden window-shades, cool cane chairs, silk Thai pillows, and boat-shaped peddles all form

unchangeable Thai scenery in the guest room, where the native culture and life is available at hand.

Influenced by Indian Buddhism and Brahmanism, the culture of Thailand has a strong sense of religion, which can be found in the drop lights and the colorful carpet in the corridor.

Ascending upstairs to the top roof, we can hear the whispering of the autumn uttered by four wooden carvings.

Furniture Design and Materials

An entire landscape glass wall comes into view as we are stepping into the sitting room, where the interior daylight and the exterior green plants are perfectly integrated. The soul of the sitting room decoration lies in wood. The Southeast Asian woodcraft is interpreted from the folding ceiling of sloping roof to the folding screen, wooden flooring and chairs.

The decorative fireplace and the hanging Thai copper art works produce comfortable feelings in sight, containing some primitive fidelity and calming influence.

The taste of returning to nature and pursuing the original flavor is prolonged from the sitting room to the dining hall.

The partially opened space and exchanges of dark and light colors bring Thai elegance and prudence. Every decorative element emits the South Seas sentiments. Using Chinese hand-drawing screen, an elegant living space equipped with tropical smell and modern features is formed.

The application of materials in Southeast Asian homes is classical, elegant and unique. The integral ambiance projects Buddhist sense of tranquility and philosophy of causal life.

Leaning against the railing, we'll boast an enjoyable view of lakes and mountains and enjoy the poetic atmosphere of aquatic life.

Imperial Palace
B-type Villa

▶ European Style

As a high-end villa, Luoyang Imperial Palace is designed for clients by heart, so the designers are invited for their years of refined decoration experience in show flat. In this case, they select the natural, elegant, implicit and noble British style as the basic design, and add their own heroic dream. It would be meaningless for our existence, if there were no idealism. we feel free to be stuck in them. We always wish for the appearance of a hero who is ready to fight or even sacrifice for us, but we never consider whether we can be the hero or even we can behave as Don Quixote.

"In our heart, we are consistently longing for the knight spirit, a mix of opposite qualities—elegant, modest, mild on the one side, and rough, arrogant, courageous on the other side; rational, cautious and clearly logical outwardly but wild, passionate or impulsive inwardly. To uphold their ideal and principle, they can abandon their egos and lusts."

The case involves a three-floor villa with a basement. The basement is the host's recreational area, including a cigar bar and a wine storage. The reception room and the dining hall are on the ground floor. Because of its large area, a section of the dining hall is partitioned off for morning tea area. The secondary room and the master room are respectively on the first and the second floor.

Designers
HAN Song & YAO Qisheng
(Shenzhen Horizon Space
Design Company)

Photographer
Shenzhen Horizon Space
Design Company

Area
600m²

Materials
wood veneer/marble/
stone mosaic

Location
Luoyang, China

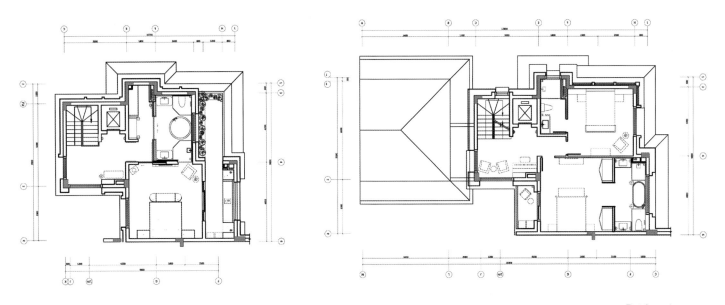

Second floor plan

First floor plan

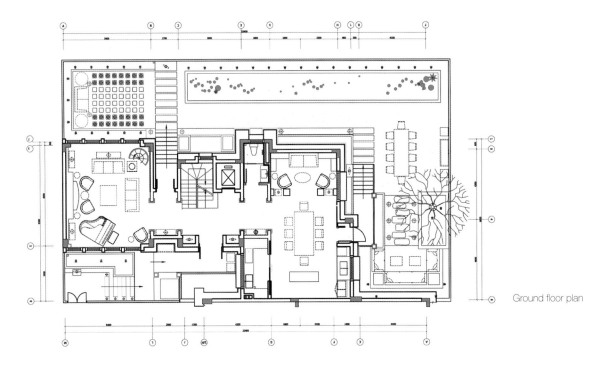

Ground floor plan

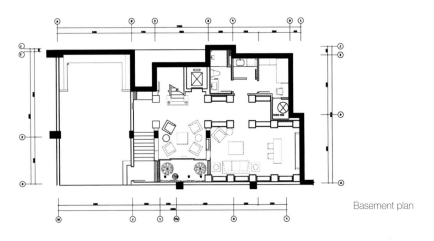

Basement plan

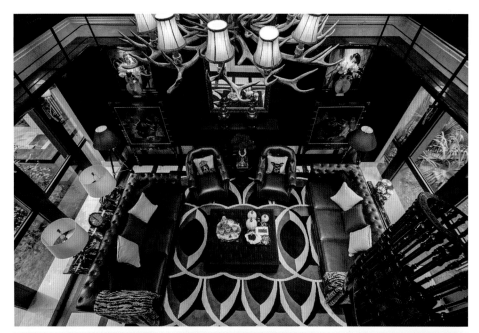

Decoration and Furnishing

The British style is adopted in the interior deign, so the hues and accessories have tough and masculine qualities. The decorative painting of horse head caters for the theme of knight spirit. Various metal accessories are the metaphor of the knight's temperament with apparent features of British style such as stripes and the union jack pattern on fabrics. Lamps wear a vintage look, bringing medieval flavor to the entire space.

Furniture Design and Materials

Leather, a symbol of nobility, is used for sofas and chairs. Most rooms use wood veneer collocated with wall lamp to increase light, and a classical atmosphere seems to be called up.

International Expo Townhouse

- A Life of the Blues under the Warm Sunshine

▶ European Style

Designer
ZHANG Li, LAI Yurui,
SI Tuyou

Photographer
ZHANG Li, LAI Yurui,
SI Tuyou

Area
363m²

Materials
white color artificial stone/
off-white gray/autumn
color paint flooring/multiply
parquet/shell mosaic

Location
Nanchang, China

As contemporary life standard is increasing, the significance of space has already surpassed the facet of material demands in real life, and reached a higher facet of spiritual pursuit. People are more likely to concern and consider about how to upgrade the understanding of space from materials to spiritual abstract, by means of which unique design qualities and artistic taste of space can be highlighted. This project presents an interior space with a mixed tastes of elegance and calmness, wisdom and modesty, modernness and novelty. Although with a distinct European style, the entire space has a distinctive charm of modern art. The visual language formed by modern graphic design has been tactfully integrated into the space, which guarantees the residents will enjoy a life of the blues under the warm sunshine in an elegant and beautiful atmosphere of art, feeling their own quiet moments. The bold application of the low-key color of gray as the background color in most space, which is assisted by lively dark as embellishment, creates a spatial feeling of brightness and simplicity. The modern, cozy and restrained design elements are integrated into the entire atmosphere in order to highlight the calm and tough, wise and profound life experiences and artistic taste, and to display the three-dimensional feeling of space and unique cultural taste. Meanwhile, it also helps the resident to pursue the perfection of life standard and comfortable dwelling. At the early stage of the design, the arrangement of space was adjusted to appropriateness and beauty in layout, connection, size, proportion and shape to satisfy the needs of functions and aesthetics. In our eyes, design is a reflection of our living conditions. It is not only for exhibition, but also offers solutions to problems of living. In this four-floor villa, each floor is independent and connected. Division between three floors and the basement is distinct: the former are for the family while the latter is for friends and business. The ground floor is designed for dining hall where enough space is retained to guarantee day lighting and cozy living. The first floor is for privacy of family members. In view of social contact, the basement is designed for private club, where friends can take drink, chat, discuss business and enjoy movies.

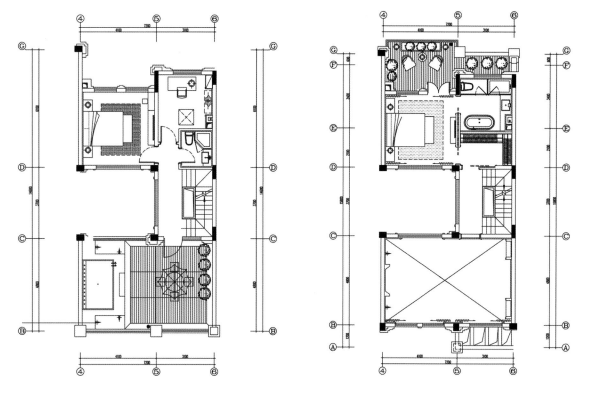

Second floor plan

First floor plan

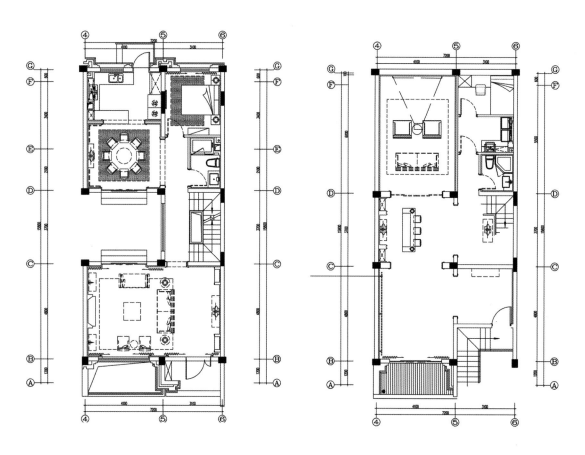

Ground floor plan

Basement plan

Decoration and Furnishing

The decoration is completed by Space Planning Imaging, who has integrated modern elements into the original style of hard pack, making the monotonous space alive. This conforms to the design theme—yuppie, a style of profound cultural ambience and pluralistic features.

If the hard pack is likened to man's body, the decoration is man's soul. They both collide and integrate with each other. The most satisfying point of the project is that modern art is brought into the entire European style, which brings perfect visual impact and lively and cozy home atmosphere.

The hanging pictures of duck, rabbit or chimpanzee are hand drawings of Spanish designer, Yago, which create a relaxed and dynamic atmosphere with delights and artistic forms. As the spotlight of space, these drawings bring distinctive home atmosphere, consistent with the client who came back from abroad with advanced education and a high level of aesthetics.

Another proof of the above is the visual impact caused by the modern art the designer brought into the strong European style. Mood varies with different decorations, emitting the power of love and new energy. Whether hanging pictures or vases, any decoration shows the client's passion for life.

Color Matching

All decorations are bespoke designs of Space Planning Imaging. The purity of blue color gives us associations of the sea, the sky, the water and the universe. The color of blue signifies beauty, calmness, reason and broadness with the meanings of braveness, calmness, reason and perseverance. The gray color gives the space quiet, prudent and harmonious feelings, adaptable to a kind of life attitude. The collision of blue and gray colors generats passion and aspiration for life.

Chengdu Zhonghai International Community Peak Villa

- Space of Warmth and Goodwill

▶ European Style

Designer
XIE Hui, ZUO Liping, SHI Lu
(X.H Interior Design)

Photographer
LI Heng

Area
400m²

Materials
antique tile/wallpaper/paint/
gray wood

Location
Chengdu, China

Because of sophistication and changeability of human nature, the understanding of "home" varies at different stages of life. But the pursuit and expectation of love and beauty is invariable, which can be collectively called "happiness" when it refers to the family and home. Happiness is a kind of feeling, and to the private house design, it does not rely on high-profile modeling or fancy decoration. Instead, designers must jump over the formal appearance of space and concentrate on the nature of life. Only by the care of humanity can happiness be attained.

In this 400m² townhouse, the seemly restrained design approach is in fact aimed to endow life with happiness and recover the nature of space through tonal control and emotional refinement.

In addition, relatively homogeneous space pattern contributes to psychological comfort which can be disturbed by imbalance in size or volume. Therefore, by rearrangement of space together with collocation of colors and display of furniture, the designers create visual changes making it possible that every small space is a homogeneous square, unblocked and sleek.

The apparent disadvantages of the dining hall are its vertical height and poor daylight due to the long distance. However, in the late reconstruction, the original disadvantages turn out to be a spotlight of the case. The designers open a pair of opposite windows on the walls of the upper bedrooms, which introduces air and light into the dining hall, and the disadvantages of breath and lighting are compensated. More importantly, this pair of opposite windows correspond with the corridor of the first floor and public area downstairs, functioning as the best place for an emotional connection in space. Thanks to variable smaller impediments and blocks, such connection is not abrupt;; instead, it has sort of oriental aesthetics flavor, making people feel pleasant and attached.

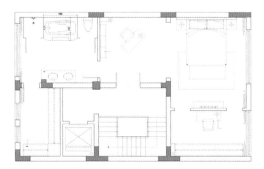

Second floor plan

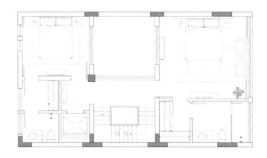

First floor plan

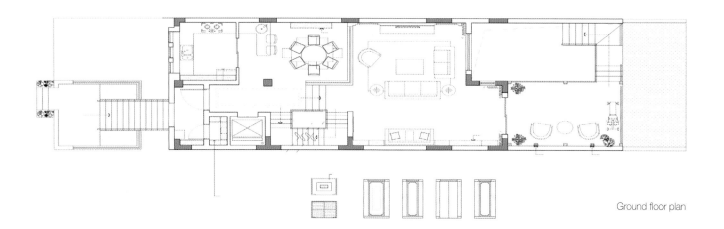

Ground floor plan

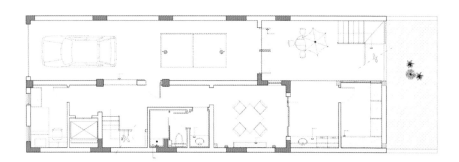

Basement plan

Decoration and Furnishing

As the center of the villa, the diversity display makes its vast empty space abundant and filled with ease. The juxtaposition of box-type tea table evolving from the loft style, cotton and linen sofa with classical Italian features, and neoclassical chairs removes individual traits and makes the space inclusive to its utmost, making visitors feel the warmth and goodwill of the host.

The master bedrooms can be quiet, simple and beautiful, with a small balcony included, which makes the space open and plain. In form, basic furnishings are reserved, showing an individual and private attitude.

In general, kid bedrooms are designed in two aspects—natural development and expected status. In this project, it is the former. Thus, there is no apparent indicators, and with the passage of time, kids grow up as they wish.

Color Matching

The tone and soul of space is decided by color. Of all colors, the neutrals are most gentle and visually perceptive with warmth in restraints. Therefore, the neutrals such as creamy white and light gray are employed in vast areas of space, together with a few golden accessories and green plants to add brightness, strength and warmth. In such space, the feeling of time turns wonderful and affectionate immediately when one is just curling up in the sofa chair, feeling the touch of gentle sunshine and breeze. The warmth extends to all functional space, coordinated and united. In generality, the designers add light colors such as green, pink and yellow or different patterns to independent space for the sake of telling individual features. They are either flexible or elegant, but maintain consistent unity and correspondence, showing the designers' adept skills in the control of colors.

House GI10

▶ European Style

Designers
HUANG Shuheng, OU Yangyi, CHEN Youru, ZHANG Huawen (Sherwood Design)

Photographer
ZHAO Zhicheng

Area
150m²

Materials
nero margiua/mirror stainless steel/silver foil / gold foil/pattern mosaic

Location
Guiyang, China

Apart from learning the basic needs of the owner, Sir HUANG Shuheng, before his design, also got to know the family experience: the owner's off-springs, in their childhood, led a vagrant life. Later, they got somewhere by chance, but still found something unsatisfactory in their life, especially the absence among family members. In her elderly time, the owner's off-springs finally realized the importance of affection after numerous experiences. Hence, they decided to reunite with their mother, as if they flew back to their childhood. In Sir HUANG Shuheng's eyes, it is abundance of mind and understanding of life that can achieve eternal well-being, rather than temporary enjoyment of life. He always holds professional aspirations that he is able to tailor design unique space for different clients in any project. As the heart and soul of the space is tempered in itself, his design works can transmit positive energy. Beauty is the combination of the interior and the exterior. Therefore, a house is supposed to have its heart and soul apart from external aesthetic. In this project, Sir HUANG Shuheng designed a high-end luxury mansion, tailored for the client, not only by variety of design terms but also thorough consideration of the owner's demands in living function. First and foremost, the huge mechanically interactive art in the sitting room, tailored for the family, is most impressive. There are two hallways in this exclusive mansion with distinct colors—black and white, which are respectively for exterior and interior hallways. The binary opposition theory is strictly adhered to throughout the mansion, demonstrating among sections, deep or shallow, big or small, high or low, etc. As the theory of Yin-Yang in Chinese metaphysics, the oppositions inter-transmit supplementary and co-existent energy. Apart from the division of depth and shallowness, the individual region of each family member is specifically designed in order to highlight public and private areas. The master bedroom, the study, the dressing room and the bathroom of one member, for example, are presented in reversible lines without impediments of doors, which constitutes independent space. For Sir HUANG Shuheng, the design principle is supposed to be human-oriented, and via the infusion of combination of well-being, the design offers a blueprint of happy life. For the convenience of caring for the senior, a special room is designed in the space next to the children's individual regions.

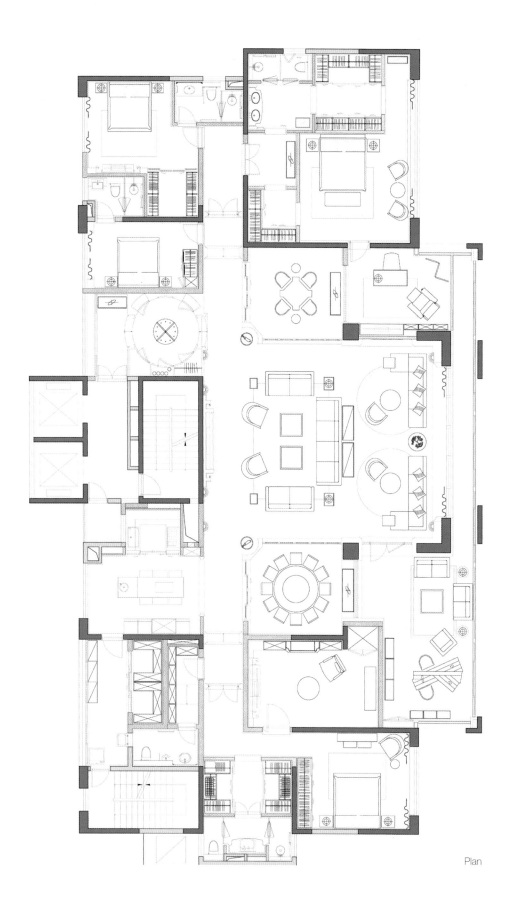

Plan

Decoration and Furnishing

There is a lively statue at the exterior hallway, a symbol of vitality of the mansion. As we approach the interior hallway, dramatic tension and visual impact are brought to us by the crystal ceiling lamp and a variety of colors.

Due to the owner's preference for European classical style, the sitting room has dominant colors of black, white and silver, coupled with rich colors to create visual focus. The proportion of colors is either introverted or extroverted, and thus, a sense of dignity and magnificence, instead of sumptuous or vulgar qualities is created. The sitting room is divided into two

sections, of which the front caters for guests, where a floral pattern carpet in combination with bespoke white sofa manifests grandness, and the back is designed for a wide range of functions.

Unlike the process of selecting art works for customers, Sir HUANG Shuheng, with his years of study of mechanism and interactive devices, cooperated with Sir XI Shibin and they artistically created a large flower-shaped mechanical installation on the ceiling of the sitting room.

The appearance of the installation is taken

from silver ornaments of the Miao (an ethnic group). With the image of iris, the core of the installation is covered by winding and gorgeous flower-shaped ornaments embedded with colored glasses at intervals. Much as the rotation of planets and stars, the huge feather-shaped silver circle will rotate around the core slowly when the installation starts, and so do the flowers on the circle. This is an analogy of parental-child relationship: whatever the distance is, the children propelled by kind of gravity are supposed to return and to be with their mother, never to be separated.

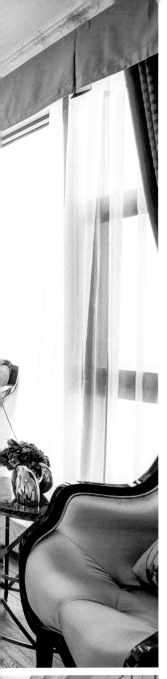

In the master's bedroom, simple linear panels extend from the ceiling to the bed back, forming a delightful contrast with the floral patterns on the gold violet carpet. The crystal wall lamps glow, adding elegance and nobility to the owner.

Meanwhile, in view of safety, handrails are installed in bedrooms and bathrooms.

Particularly, in case of accidents, abrasive flooring and shower seats are set in bathrooms where proper adjustment is made for convenient access and maintenance.

Due to the preference of a family member for oriental art, the design of the study exhibits elegance of the oriental literati, with bespoke manual wallpaper of Hermes .

Furniture Design and Materials

The living room is most different from the sitting room in design features, where simple and neat lines outline a modern, elegant and classic style. Tranquility, the essential element of life, is expressed by simple and introverted space. In the living room, the owner can meditate, sipping hot tea while gazing into the landscape through window, as if he could embrace the universe. The flooring of the dining hall is in hexagons,

similar to those of chessboard. Embellished with a faint of golden yellow, the back of chairs are delicately engraved, exhibiting the apparent contrast between simplicity and complexity of modern Baroque style. Likewise, the chess room, with a single color, exhibits low-key luxury by the display of delicate and exquisite ornaments made of gold or silver .

Apart from the master bedroom, study, the dressing room and the bathroom, the private areas include a cigar lounge, where quiet and leisure space for the inner world is created by mysterious ancient royal cellar atmosphere. The cigar lounge also serves as an audiovisual room, where people not only enjoy cigars but also have sensory enjoyment.

Between Mountain and Sea

▶ European Style

Designers
PANG Yifei, YUAN Yi,
ZHANG Qian, XIA Tingting
(PinChen Design)

Photographer
PinChen Design, Chongqing

Area
180m²

Materials
antique solid wood flooring/
diatom mud/willow veneer/
the Aegean Sea gray stones/
linen fabric

Location
Dali, China

Located in the tranquil Dali Ancient Town, this project is the very definition of winter sunshine, sunbathing with dessert or enjoying birds soaring into the cloud, and we are simply satisfied with the gaze into the cozy atmosphere. The faint images of a wisp of smoke and boating on the Erhai Lake are peculiar to Dali, where the absence of visitor's disturbance leaves people to appreciate in tranquility.

This villa is endowed with exquisite temperament because of its unique geographical advantage, and naturally it opts for resort style. As a poetic dwelling house located in the mountains and alongside the Erhai Lake, the villa is worthy of its name—Between Mountain and Sea. The designer set the theme of the project as "ideal approach and tranquil living", which indicates the mutuality of ideals and living: the ideal is living in tranquility and in turn, tranquil living makes the ideal more approachable. Apparently, Dali, the enchanted ancient town, deserves such poetic life.

Have an ideal afternoon and enjoy leisure's company when you're taking a walk. Shop at the local market, select food and prepare a substantial meal for relatives or friends in person, and you will find a realm you've failed to notice in daily life, and generate a great many lively inspirations.

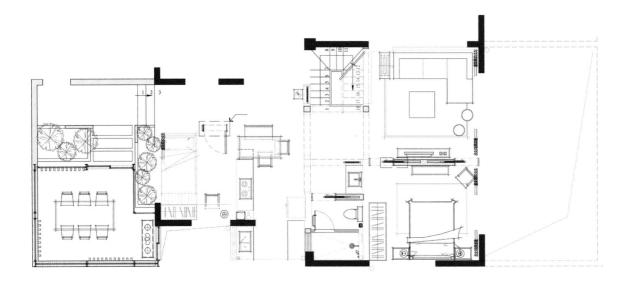

Ground floor plan

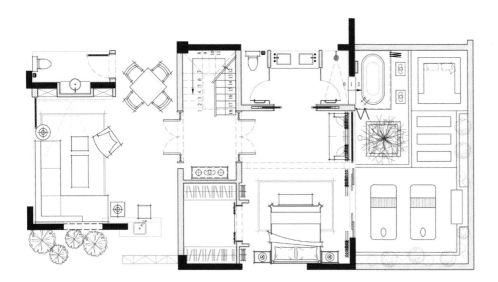

Basement plan

Decoration and Furnishing

Bespoke Persian carpet, sheep leather manual lamp and warm color light in the room make people like staying inside. The antique solid wood flooring, willow veneer and linen fabric make the room filled up with the flavor of old times. For residents in Dali Ancient Town, the ever-increasing expectations gradually undermine their original fresh feeling; thus the interior of the house needs to assimilate novelties, and be memorable to the dwellers for a decade or more by its purity, plainness and feelings of past life.

Furniture Design and Materials

The project is a house with three bedrooms, three living rooms and three bathrooms. The first floor is arranged for living room, guest bedroom, kids' room and kitchen. The ground floor is arranged for master bedroom and entertainment. There is a spacious cloakroom in the master bedroom, which is the highlight of the overall space. Fat distant from the normal damp look, the ground floor is designed for the master's room. The designer deliberately restores spatial relationships, aiming to have the visible and tender beams of sunlight penetrating into the room.

Buena Vista

▶ European Style

Interior Design and
Decoration
Eric Tai Design Co., Ltd.

Photographer
CHEN Weizhong

Area
810m²

Completion
2015

Materials
Jobs marble/creamy white
colored marble/imitation
brick/walnut solid flooring/
latex paint/KOHLER/
cupboard/Bose

Location
Shanghai, China

Buena Vista is a good example of minimalist design approach, which reminds people of Ludwig Mies Van der Rohe, the priest of modernist architecture whose deign philosophy is "less is more". In the early 1930s, Mies was living in a similar social environment where the storm of designs was overwhelming and these people found nothing more than old-fashioned patterns could demonstrate magnificence. Therefore, Chateau de Versailles, Schloss Burg an Der Wupper (in the 18th century) or rural houses (under the Tudors or during the George era) were intentionally imitated in most luxurious residence designs. The copies were not the refinements of the aesthetics; instead they are closely associated with implications of authority and superiority. But it was Mies who tailored an elegant modern palace for a couple with the design philosophy of "less is more" and redefined the standard of luxury, which altered the aesthetics the old aristocracy relied on, and certified that affluence can even forecast the future besides owning a fashionable look. Will Eric Tai's future designs be labeled "less is more"? Eric Tai interpreted his design concept of Buena Vista as the following: the process of design is also a course of gradual understanding of oneself. And after selections, the integration of Chinese and Western elements is in favor, and the longing for plain, delicate, elegant and dignified home space is reinforced. He also clearly sets forth his concept of elegance: it is a decent and delicate appearance; it is a rich and powerful inner world; it is a specific character, gentle but not too soft, strong but not too severe; it is a positive attitude towards life, easy and calm. The interior of the villa covers 580m² , and in total, the garden and the balcony cover 230m². The interior space is magnificent and the function is perfect. There are five bedrooms and six luxurious bathrooms. Besides independent and spacious sitting room and dining hall, the villa is also equipped with family room, reading room, billiards, fitting area, bar and multi-function hall. Well-designed garden is planned for green plants by professional landscape companies, and carefully planted flowers such as mangnolia and bougainvillea. are vibrant and lively. There is a basketball court on the ground floor of the garden.

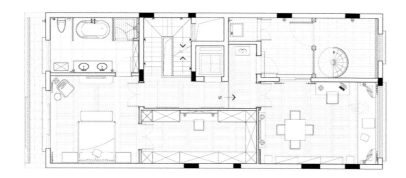

Second floor plan

First floor plan

Ground floor plan

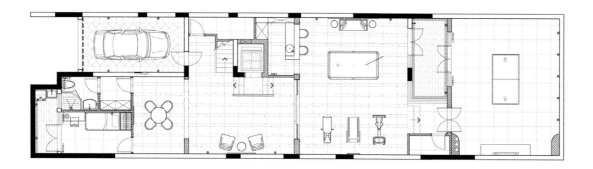

Basement plan

Decoration and Furnishing

In simple and cozy space, candlesticks, simple
and plain flower decorations and books on
art, fashion, architecture and literature are
omnipresent.

144

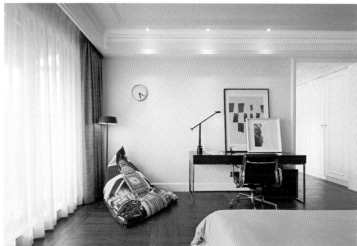

Furniture Design and Materials

Walls of fireplace, TV and headboard are paneled in white-wired frames made of excellent environmentally friendly materials and paint. In view of the wet climate of the South, the designers use colorful latex paint to replace wallpapers. Thus, light gray covers vast area; icy gray is for the sports area; pale green is for the study and blue is for kid room. Atmospheres of different space are defined by colors. Under the white tone, creamy white imitation brick is easier to maintain with stone-like texture. The purple red solid flooring of the bedroom forms a distinct contrast between dark and light colors, making the interior fashionable and bright. The ceiling is edged with simple plaster lines. Most simple neoclassical styled furniture is made from walnut and rosewood with a few Chinese styled furniture as embellishments, such as side table,

tea table with armchair, and meditation chair, bringing out an atmosphere of humanism. In the kid room, Thomas bed is bought in Hongkong, and other furniture is from IKEA. Eric Tai: "I like reading, so basically, I hope to offer people a sense of quietness in my interior designs, which are suitable for reading and rest. It is pleasant to spend more time reading." Indeed, on the ground floor, books and picture albums are stacked on the huge coffee table (1.4m×1.4m) and bar counter; on the first floor, bookcases are indispensable in both sitting room and kid room; on the second floor, not only bookcases but also tea chairs and sofas are served for leisure reading.

Color Matching

Contrast to his usual designs which leave people an impression of Chinese elegance, Eric Tai employs pure white color in Buena Vista. He uses minimal lines to interpret his concept of order and limitation in the hope of creating a spacious home space. So the vast area of pure white is the presentation of the longing for a pure world. A few shades of icy gray, pale gray and cornflower blue are added in accordance with functional features. The juxtaposition of European and Chinese styles forms a visual paradox, making diversity possible.

Lin Xi Bay Model Villa

▶European Style

Designer
KKD Design Co., Ltd.

Photographer
KKD Marketing Department

Area
330m²

Materials
Lounge bar: marble
Sitting room wall: yellow
colored glass steel/tawny
glass
Veneer: antique oak
Master bathroom: Hoary
white-grained marble
Brands:
Fabric: Shenzhen Lavida
Furnishing Material
Flooring: Steinbache
Stone: KANGLI

Location
Zhengzhou, China

Any designer may sometimes be confronted with sticky situation where their reputation can be damaged or even ruined by certain project. But this is not true of Kenneth Ko who prefers to challenge, and Lin Xi Bay Model Villa, a medium house type of town houses and a problem to any designer, is just one of such projects, whose final design effects gain a big round of applause for KKD.

Lin Xi Bay Model Villa is a high-end project by Xinxing Real Estate. Canada's ADS Architecture Design Company is in charge of the architectural design, landscape is by Belt Collins, Hong kong, and KKD is responsible for the interior design. The concept of simple luxury is interpreted by metropolis style, the representative of urban life taste, which aims to increase the a Villa's value by extreme control of living details. Settle down in Lin Xi Bay and you'll enjoy the simple luxury of life.

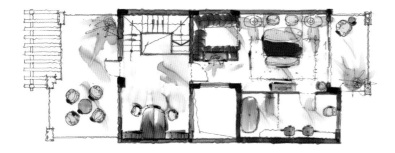

Second floor plan

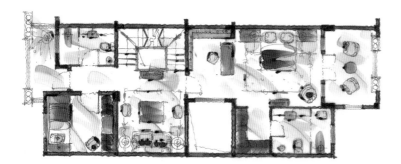

First floor plan

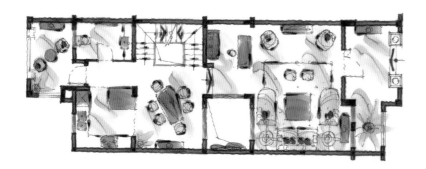

Ground floor plan

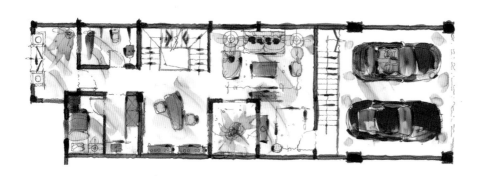

Basement plan

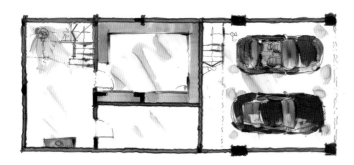

B2 plan

Decoration and Furnishing

Light-hue furniture in the dining hall on the ground floor endows fine spatial perception and pure vision. The use of large pieces of glass and the metal mirror breaks original sections in space. The sitting room, the dining hall, the kitchen, and the light well are integral. The embellishment of international furniture, ornaments, pendants and precious marbles create a sense of texture in the interior, exhibiting living details, worth savoring.

The leisure household tenor is expressed via crystal lamps, high-quality furniture, avant-garde brilliant metal art wares, together with a large cloakroom.

Lin Xi Bay is an architecture of three floors above ground and two basements. The brilliant drop lights make the staircase an artistic connection of these five floors. Stepping from the study on the top floor to the leisure hall on basement 2, anyone can feel as if they were wandering through the long river of history. Immersed in humanity flavor, every detail in the space is the interpretation of elegance.

Furniture Design and Materials

The design of the kid room on the first floor takes the theme of flight. Hand-drawing, the representative design approach, together with actual wood propeller forms a theme wall, a salute to the classic fairy tale "The Little Prince", and a return to childhood of fancies and adventures.

Integrated wardrobe and desk saves space, and the tatami near the window satisfies kids' longing for stars.

The first floor is for the seniors, where the barrier-free design makes the study, the bedroom and the leisure balcony all together form a small life circle. Even indoors, the elderly people can enjoy the tranquility of peaceful life.

Indented glass wall is built on the entry into the master bedroom on the second floor, which adds to the confined space a more comfortable extension.

Outside the study is a private terrace. The woven-back pure white soft chairs have holiday feelings, suitable for chat and spiritual release.

At night, lighting candles can add sort of romance here. Here, the nearest place to the sky, seas of trouble recede and the pretty look of life emerges afterwards.

The combination of acrylic and raw wood forms the contrast between roughness and delicateness, primitiveness and modernity— opposite and united in one body as two aspects. KKD explores more of the extension and diversity of cultural essence in space.

Color Matching

To display metropolitan romantic odor and beautiful connotation, the hallway, the leisure hall, and the wine cellar are emphasized by color weaving and mixing in contrast to the plain and elegant background, exhibiting a casual lifestyle.

The vibrant colors of sunflower yellow, orange, sea blue and wine red are all like the dreamland woven by desires and dreams which kindles inner world passions and fantasies.

The plain and warm decorative hue creates pleasant and comfortable environment for rest, and guarantees good sleep for the seniors every night.

With corresponding colors to light the entire space, the design elements are appropriately displayed, while the gorgeous colors of the inner world are the after-drinking kaleidoscope.

Luxury Barn Living

▶ Modern Simplicity
   Style

Designers
HUANG Shihua, MENG Yiwen,
YUAN Xiaoyuan, WANG
Zhiliang, SU Peixuan, PANG
Bingwei (XY Interior Design
Consultant Co.,Ltd.)

Photographer
CEN Xiuxian

Area
780m²

Materials
1F
Italian stone plate
(1500×3000mm)/Italian stone
tie/white paint/transparent
granite plate/Ti-stainless
steel/white arificial stone/
Clean Up kitchenware
(Janpanese)
2F
platane wood/white artificial
stone/walnut floor (Narrow,
W:50mm,H: 25mm)/leather-
stripped paint/ stucco/granite
flake/black brick/Pandomo/
calfskin/black Ti-stainless
steel/brushed stainless steel
(5mm)/gray paint glass/Italian
wood brick/ Italian concrete
brick/JØTUL/cast tron
fireplace
3F
rubber floor/strengthened
floating floor/mirror (5mm)/
brushed stainless steel/
blackboard paint/cement
paint/white paint/light brown
paint/walnut floor (Broad)

Location
Taoyuan,Taiwan, China

The client, an after-80s athlete who likes movie, music and competitive sports in particular, used to live in Vancouver, Canada, and later came back and settled down in Taoyuan city.

The architecture inherits North American style, and does not lay emphasis on residential luxury or modeling complexity. Integrated with landscape, the architecture is designed for texture presentation. Tight-knit but comfortable landscape surrounds the architecture, and American minimalist window frames, together with roofs, well connect tenderness and crudeness. There flows spring water into the cascading pool located in the southeastern corner. The constant spring water, thus, forms a small-sized biological circulation system for fish and water plants. In a word, all designs are closely associated with life.

The first floor is arranged for living room, study and bedroom. Without complex shapes or disturbing light, the master bedroom is the extension of the living room, functioning as a recreational area as well. Another living center on this floor is the bathroom located in the master bedroom, which consists of a double shower cubicle compatible with steam room, double bathtub and double washbasin.

On the second floor is a five-star professional fitness center. Weight training section, comprehensive training section, dancing practice section and guest rooms are set here.

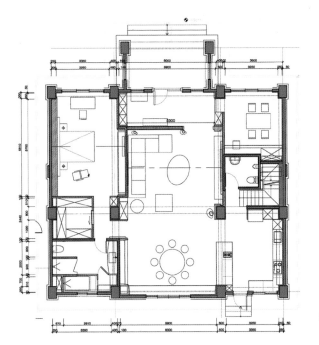

Second floor plan

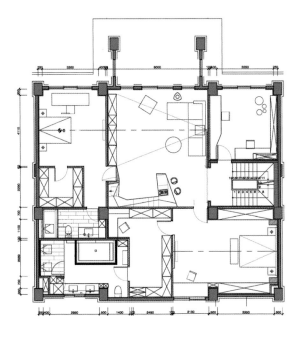

First floor plan

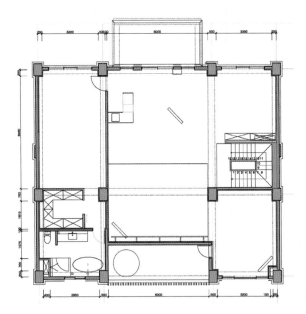

Ground floor plan

Decoration and Furnishing

Ventilation pipes are placed in every part of the architecture. With double slanted roofs serving as ventilation transformation layer, the chimney effect is adopted in the design. The architecture can self-regulate temperature with a central ventilation system. The ground floor is the extension of the architecture's minimalist American lifestyle. The huge lobby protects the resident's privacy and welcomes visitors by works of art. On the first floor, the cast iron fireplace is loaded with the owner's memory of Vancouver life. Here, the concept of primitive living in nature is defined as a balance achieved by seeking for details, rather than crudeness alone. Before you enter Barn Living, a barn door is right in front of your eyes, which is in sharp contrast with its post wrapped with embedded geometrical shapes. Indefinite arrangement of TV walls or furniture is the presentation of the concept of lounge, which creates a sense of casualness and coziness.

Furniture Design and Materials

The magnificence of the architecture is displayed by cut surface stones (80mm) collocated with rough surface stones. Tainwan local black oak wood plays a leading role in the landscape.

The barn door on the first floor, and black bricks and processed platane wood create a strong flavor. The lounge is still in geometrical style. Burly wood is in contrast with antique wood, forming a flavor of life. The bar counter is compatible with gathering and domestic use. The dark colored background wall of the independent fireplace is built in correspondence with the texture of antique black bricks. The designers create the impression that the space is free from decoration by deliberately leaving brick joints unfilled and processed platane wood, and thus the trace of time is retained. The gloss of feather-grained PANODOMO flooring makes sense of depth. The shape of substantial soft colored leather bag promises high-quality sleep. The logs at both sides fill up the space with warmth and softness. Painted ceiling and cement-like stucco add details to crudeness. The dressing room is shaped in leather and Ti-stainless steel, which is intended to lift the ground level to avoid dampness.

Considering temperature maintenance and drainage mechanism, the bathtub is diamond-shaped. The washbasin is made from brushed stainless steel (5mm) in collaboration with concrete bricks. The second floor is designed in recent CROSS FIT style. The iron gray rubber floor has a weight capacity of 300 kg. The bar counter is made of stainless steel. Apart from the function of heat dissipation, the door plank with punched holes contains sports elements. The walls are decorated with huge mirror coupled with stainless steels, and the original ceiling is in cement coating.

Color Matching

The study on the first floor is also the place for drum practice. Thus, it is integrated with rock and roll elements—metal in collocation with leather and dark colors. Moreover, functions like sound insulation, absorption and reduction are also taken into account. The guest room is in minimalist American style with strong colors. The contrast between antique violet and white colors, and the soft colored leather bags at the headboard and the tail stock add romance to the space. Besides, the white dressing room and finely designed bathroom create a sense of living. The guest room on the second floor is also in minimalist American style with warm colored rooms and bathrooms, highlighting the atmosphere of life.

City Valley Villa

▶ Modern Simplicity
Style

Designers
PENG Zheng, CHEN Yongxia,
LI Yonghua (C&C Design)

Photographer
C&C Design

Area
320m^2

Materials
marble/solid wood flooring/
paint panel/hard pack/
stainless steel/wallpaper

Location
Dongguan, China

This project, targeted at Dongguan and Shenzhen customers, is a town house. City Valley Villa is located in Qingxi town, the border of two cities, Dongguan and Shenzhen in Guangdong Province. Enjoying unique landscape resource, Qingxi town is a flower blossom place. On the theme of "idle life in the sunshine", the design is expected to give a full display for the advantages of the project, such as geographic position, dwelling size, etc.

Tired of the bustling urban life, we need something simple and tranquil. Having abandoned complicated ornaments, exaggerated manners and showy colors, the design maintains agreeable manners, lively colors, elegant textures and imaginable emptiness. In the afternoon, the gentle breeze is blowing with endless sunshine and scent of soil coming towards us...

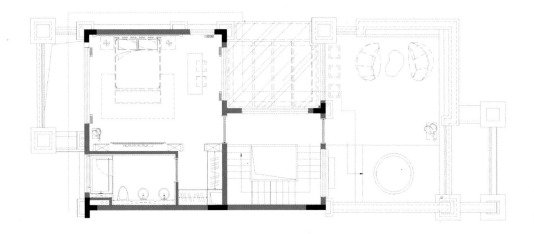

Second floor plan

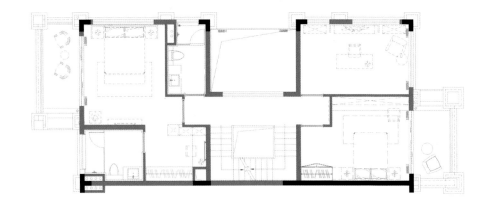

First floor plan

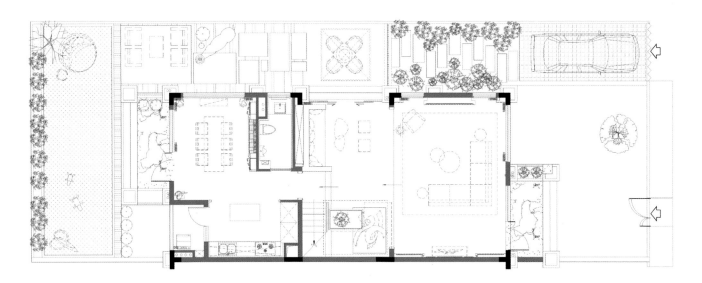

Ground floor plan

Decoration and Furnishing

The living room on the ground floor is simple, bathing the abundant bright sunshine. The interior and the exterior space is effectively interactive through the arrangement of life scenes. The extended sun room is an important living space for individualism, connecting give the living room and dining hall.

Elegance is outlined by white sofa and the curtains, and black leather armchairs make the overall space alive. Ornaments on theirregularly shaped tea table add sort of charm to the space in the subtleties. The gentle

sunshine sheds light on the living room, which appropriately interprets the design theme—idle life in the sunshine.

Also, the dining hall boasts natural sunshine. In comparison with elegance and tenderness of the living room, the white cocktail cabinet and the table with black top render the dining hall a sense of fashion.

The design of the master bedroom and bathroom is the extension of the elegant style of the living room. Fashion and coziness—simple but comfortable bed wares, and bright and dry

bathroom accessories alleviate the tension and pressure of urban life, achieving relaxed vision while satisfying the housing demand.

The master bedroom on the top floor has an independent cloakroom, a mini bar counter and a roof deck with a massage bathtub where one can enjoy the sunshine.

Hongwei Haiyi Bay

▶ Modern Simplicity
   Style

If the interior design is likened to an intriguing movie, the furniture design is the soundtrack or musical interlude, essential to the movie. It is true of household ornaments, of which decorations set the style while furnishings balance color, pattern, light and shade, and size, etc, bringing pleasant feelings of coziness and luxury.

Simplicity is not equal to plainness, and when it is confronted with luxury, it is interpreted as a low-key way to present luxury. The magnificence is embodied in details, and it usually contains more connotations and flavors. Therefore, classic and simple design elements, sumptuous hues and material textures are perfectly integrated, which interprets the resident's attitude towards life—pursuing high quality while advocating simplicity, in a reasonable and sensible way.

Designer
ZHU Junxiang
(Vita Space Design)

Area
160m²

Project Cost
1,200,000RMB

Materials
rose gold stainless steel/
marble tile/leather/ wall
covering

Location
Shenzhen, China

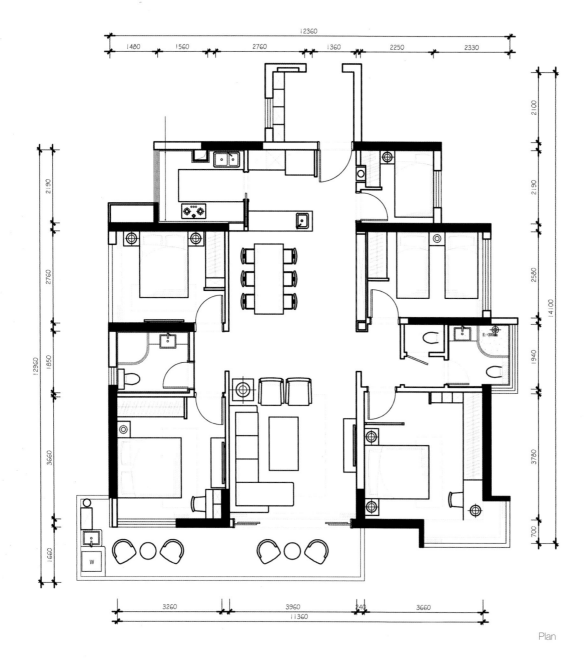

Plan

The dominant tone of the bedrooms is beige, in which the selected wallpaper, the warm bedding and fine ornaments, plus soft lighting, create a cozy and comfortable atmosphere. In the kid room, the pink color walls, the gorgeous bed curtains, the bed for princess and the furnishing sfilled with child interest all create a romantic world.

Furniture Design and Materials

A distinctively designed niche is placed at the hallway of the entrance, on which metal works of art are displayed as a prelude of inner space. The same element is applied in the wine cabinet and TV wall, simple and natural. The sofas are in dark colors, and are thus matched with ornaments and pillows in bright orange color, calm and fascinating. The entire ceiling is in folded modeling coupled with narrow champagne-gold colored stainless steel, magnificent and delicate. Natural wooden color renders the interior filled with leisure atmosphere as a rest harbor of the fast tempo urban life.

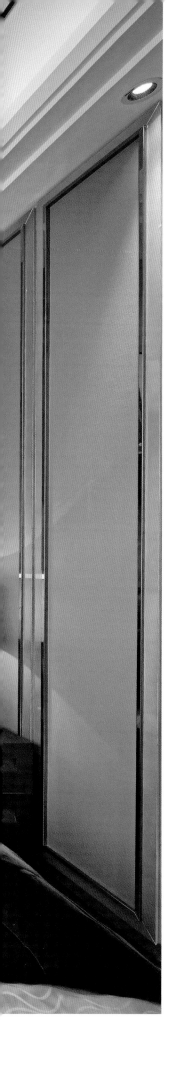

Color Matching

The luxurious space features contours in the champagne-gold color, simple and modern with good quality. At first glance, it is magnificent and simple, but when you take a second look, it is finely designed with details. Therefore, an up-to-date space with good taste, high quality and simplicity is created.

Golden Leaf Island Villa

▶ Modern Simplicity
  Style

In this project, simplicity and coziness are what the client demands, which is hard to realize in such a huge villa. Nowadays, it is precious to have a simple residence, especially in a noisy city.

Surreal Design team takes simplicity as its design theme, and manifests client's taste and life attitude via comfortable and simple residence in noisy environment. Meanwhile, Surreal Design team infuses exclusive style in the design, creating a residence filled with emotional memories and personal touch.

The project is a three-floor villa. The height of the sitting room on the ground floor reaches 6m. On the right side of the sitting room stands a mini-bar as the entertainment area. Bedrooms on the first floor contain individual bathroom. The second floor is for the owner, including cloakroom, study, storage and balcony apart from the master bedroom.

Designer
GUO Maosheng (Shenzhen
Surreal Arch Design
Consultant Co., Ltd.)

Photographer
WU Qirui

Area
530m²

Materials
cement brick/steel//latex
paint

Location
Shantou, China

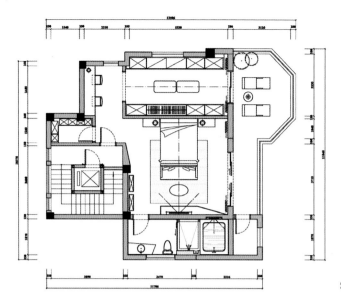

Second floor plan

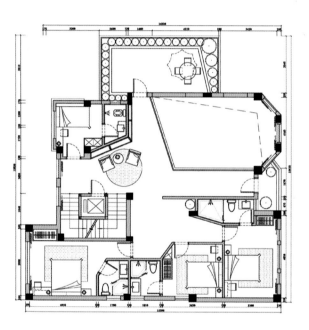

First floor plan

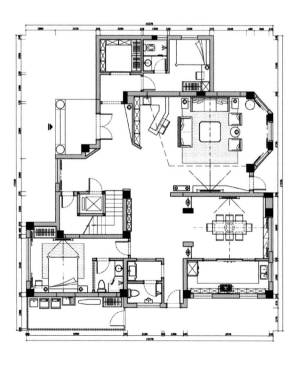

Ground floor plan

Decoration and Furnishing

The furnishing features simplicity. Thus, the sitting room is equipped with several simply shaped drop lights, rather than the normally used chandelier. The main background wall is only decorated with a paint. The dining hall follows the style of the bedroom, which features grayish white color with few bright decoration.

Furniture Design and Materials

Vast emptiness is preserved in the design, collocated with craft of paint, iron art, glass, stone, wood, etc. The space gives full play of materials and therefore forms exquisite space, exhibiting individual flavor. It attaches importance to the visual sense of beauty and practicability as well, creating co-relations among space, nature and man, and builds the simple and cozy life the client demands.

Overview/Scere

▶ Modern Simplicity
Style

The project is a four-floor villa with four bedrooms, four sitting rooms and four bathrooms. It has a capacity of 4-6 persons and adopts modern simplicity style favored by TANG Zhonghan, the designer of DA. Interior.

Overview/Scene is the theme of the design. A deliberate use of body's penetration or partially open manner, which in addition to an oppressive perception of body giving to the public, also connects and extends the vision throughout each space.With penetration through the body to observe external natural environment, environment, light and shadow consequently change with physical structures, bringing different scenes of life experiences.

It uses solid walls staggering with bodies, through a process from the master bedroom into the master bathroom; due to placement of bodies, in addition to a grant of physical function, it also uses spatial segmentation cleverly, which forms a corridor space, also a locker room. With the possibility of allocation behind different spaces, it defines field and energizes people's moving lines in space.

Distanced view in a glance spatial framing takes the environment forms a coexistence with the structure, a harmonious state with nature.This is a lifestyle we can understand; it is life space based on environment and base conditions, with the use of construction techniques forming relationship with natural environment.

Designer
TANG Zhonghan
(DA. Interior)

Photographer
Kyle Yu (DA. Interior)

Area
548m²

Materials
stone/iron/glass/PVD/
veneer/panDOMO

Location
New Taipei City, Taiwan,
China

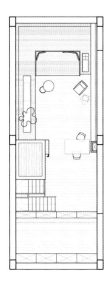

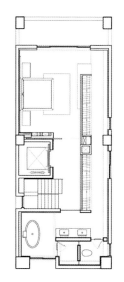

Third floor plan

Second floor plan

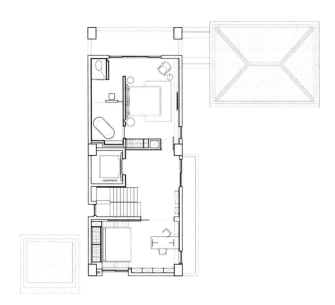

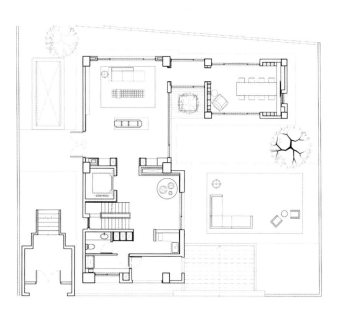

First floor plan

Ground floor plan

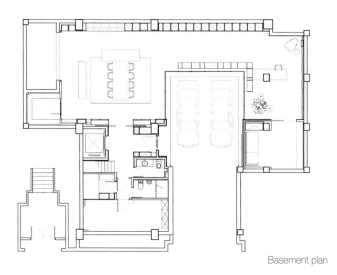

Basement plan

Decoration and Furnishing

The abstract shelves display collections and memories as well: inviting and making friends, chatting all day long with good wine, etc. Passion for music and film appreciation seem independent but in reality, are closely connected. From this moment, dreams take off.

The space atmosphere comes from demands of life, such as dreaming of an antique car symbolizes one's taste or having a big long table for banquet needs. Attic space, a memory of childhood, is mysterious and full of fantasy.

Going upstairs, all dreams and memories are presented in the real scenes of world step by step. Sitting or lying, reading or taking rests, it forms another small world at home; hence, it is eventually a perfect realization of dream.

Color Matching

Color in the natural environment comes from light and color in a space comes from materials. It uses materials' own textures and colors, which endows a new life to the modeling. With the integration of light and environment, the bathroom is designed to create a casual and relaxed atmosphere. With this, we feel cleansed of our sins and reach the inner peace.

National Gallery of Guo Mansion

▶ Modern Fashion
   Style

Designers
Eva Yuan, Carrie Meng, Mac
Huang (XY Interior Design
Consultant Co., Ltd.)

Photographer
LU Chenyu

Area
200m²

Materials
Italian marble/Iran marble/
Turkish marble/teak/walnut
wood flooring/enforced paint
glass/black mirror/oak/
white paint/white alligator
leather

Location
Taiwan, China

Conditioned to the habit developed in Los Angeles, the client, who has lived there for ten years, demands a bigger-sized kitchen. To set the design orientation, the designers spent long time on the project communicating with the client. At the beginning, they hope to create a sense of space with good taste by omitting complex decoration, and enable life to return to nature underlying in beams of light, dynamic lines and textures.

As a relaxing and comforting private residence, the mansion integrates habitation and taste and creates the highest quality of taste.

The large space of emptiness allows inhabitants to infuse their self spirit. Through personal collection, ways of furnishings, etc, the design makes space subordinate to inhabitants. The design concept of the mansion lies in beams of light, dynamic lines and textures, which are exhibited in causal elements and color matches.

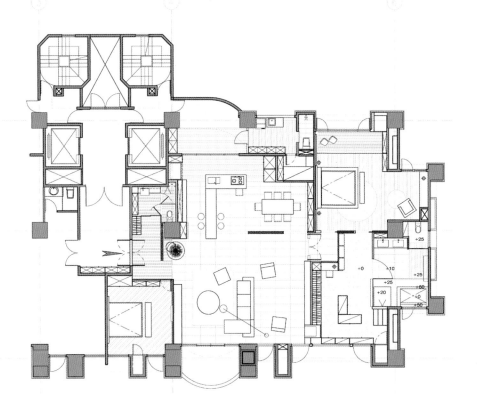

Plan

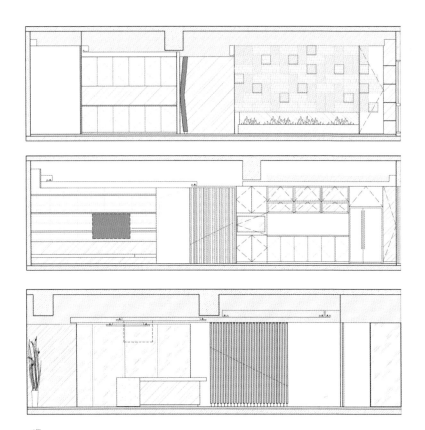

Elevations

1/30

Decoration and Furnishing

The apparatus cabinet beside the dining table is inserted with a television at its center, which helps the owner watch culinary teaching or news while cooking. The Iran marble of the TV-wall is divided by black iron. Thus, the proportion between black and white in a narrow scope is the only linear space in this romantic and sensual the mansion where the owner's taste of quality finds good expression in simplicity. On the other side, mosaic tiles and dichromatic alligator grains are the accumulation of sensibility with an open fireplace below, functioning as the lounge area. The television embedded in the bathroom cabinet gives the owner easy access to the morning or evening news.

Texture is emphasized in the selection of accessories. Floor lamps and table lamps from famous designers coordinate with leather sofas. On the balcony hangs cane chairs in which people enjoy the 101 scenery. The proper light of the guest bedroom makes people forget the urban tension immediately. The wall lamps on both sides make contrasts in space.

Furniture Design and Materials

Corresponding to the sitting room and the lounge area, the kitchen is integrated with the dining hall with a middle partition of folded wooden grid, of which the faint visual effect makes the space alive. Shades are projected regularly through the grid, which permits free flow of light along with figures and sunbeams, and forms cozy space. The design of ceiling aims to maintain the height and full range of lighting. The master bedroom seems to be the presentation of the owner's inner world, which features white color space, the symbol of feminine purity, since people, rather than materials, play a dominant role in space. The veneer provides mellow quality in conflict with the cold feeling provided by Italian marbles. Folded wooden grid is used to separate the hallway and the kitchen.

The 45° flooring of hallway strengthens the stepping feeling. The spatial feeling varies with the ceiling and the wooden grid, and the wood flooring is also replaced with marbles when we enter into the sitting room. All of this soothes our mind by peacefulness and stability upon our return from noisy outdoors.

The fiber optic lights on the ceiling, a glowing galaxy, present the owner's romantic personality.

The grid on the wall at the headboard is the continuation of modeling of public space, which also forms a casual proportion. In front of the headboard is a door plank made from white alligator leather and a white paint cabinet, which are the amazing spotlight when light is shed on the grains.

Star Wars pop art springs up when we steer into the dressing room, and on the ceiling there are Swarovski crystal lamps.

The guest room features coziness and texture with headboard in oak wooden planks and walls in light brown color.

The bathroom is set beside the hallway as a partition for the owner's privacy. The use of Turkish marble makes people visitors completely relaxed.

Victoria Harbor

▶ Modern Fashion
  Style

In the designer's eyes, a design result is sometimes fairly rational, like an answer to a math problem. Therefore, the standard of a good design should be totally customized. In this project, after comprehensive understanding of the client, a member in the fashion field, who is keen to drive sports cars and invite friends home to hold parties, Li Yizhong with his design team tailors an ideal house for the client.

This is a modern, fashionable and vibrant villa with free space, flowing air and graceful shades.

The four-floor villa has a five-floor height atrium, a basement and a roof garden.

Designers
Interior Design: LI Yizhong,
FAN Yihua, HUANG Jianfeng
(DSSY Residential Interior
Design)
Decoration: XIONG Can, OU
Xueting, SUN Bin

Area
620m²

Materials
Italian wood/walnut wood
veneer/oak flooring/bronze
stainless steel

Location
Shenzhen, China

Jasper Johns The Museum of Modern Art

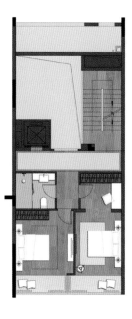

Third floor plan

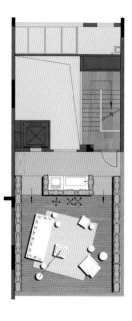

Fourth floor
plan

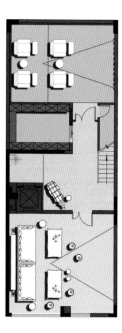

Roof terrace plan

234

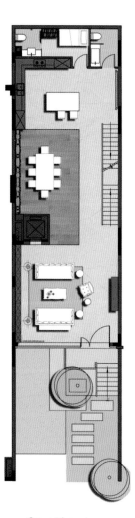

Ground floor plan

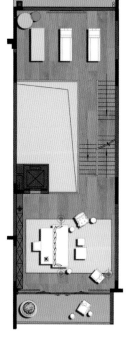

First floor plan

Second floor plan

Decoration and Furnishing

The sitting room and dining hall on the ground floor, and the tea room and audiovisual room at the basement offer hospitable space where anyone can let their feelings bubble up. In the atrium, the design of vertical greening adjusts the air quality and is most enjoyable. Through the skylight, the pouring sunlight sheds on every oily shinning leaf, permeating the breath of life. The vertical greening wall, romantic and gorgeous, serves as the spotlight of the villa.

To resolve the problem of vertical transportation, elevator is added. The atrium is at the center of the villa, from where each functional section extends. The design of the elevator brings up-down dynamics to the atrium.

The fitness room and the master study are on the first floor. The study is open, where close friends are invited and served as distinguished guests to enjoy the music over the tea chat.

Color Matching

The bedrooms are on the second and the third floor. The master bedroom is on the top, enjoying perfect view and lighting. Separated but continuous bath suites adopt the same tone as that of the bedrooms. The quiet and pure white color under the gentle lighting isolates the space from outside bustling.

Portofino Swan Castle

▶ Modern Luxury
  Style

Designer
ZHU Junxiang
(Vita Space Design)

Decoration Designer
ZHONG Xuan

Area
230m²

Cost
1,500,000 RMB

Materials
rose gold stainless steel/
Pacific gray marble/light
gray marble/Italian portopo/
China's marble/leather/
ebony/wall covering

Location
Shenzhen, China

The client is a graduate of automation major, who has long been working on the design of industrial automation products. With a distinctive eye for aesthetics, the designer is bored with his professional job, and he tends to have a place of lively atmosphere and high quality.

With low-profile nobility as the spirit of creation, the project is neither affected nor exaggerated or bustling and noisy. In contrast, it expresses an innate sense of style in space. As Tadao Ando once said, "A luxurious home is supposed to have a tranquil feeling, touching the inner world."

Through modern minimalist style, gorgeous and dazzling colors and novel matching of materials, it currently becomes an artistic symbol of fashion design.

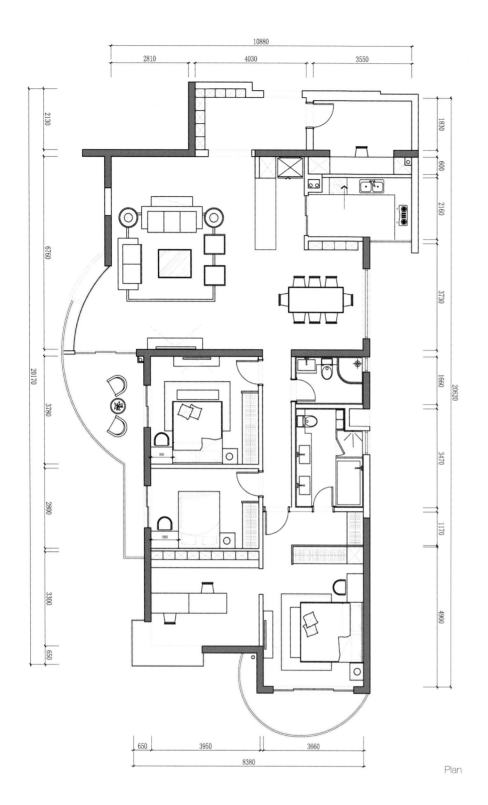

10880

2810 4030 3550

2130

6760

20170

3780

2800

3300

650

650 3950 3660

8380

1830

600

2160

3730

20620

1660

3470

1170

4900

Plan

Decoration and Furnishing

In home space design, elaborate and deluxe details reveal a highly stylized form of nature. The balance between function and beauty contributes to a comfortable, cozy and tranquil environment properly, exhibiting unspoken elegance.

The hallway is integrated into the space by vigorous visual symbols such as coverings, ornaments, furniture, etc, forming a quality derived from life but higher than it. And the artistic inspiration is omnipresent among distinctive metal lighting, coverings and artistic ornaments.

Furniture Design and Materials

Individuality and pursuit of the emerging class
finds good example in a variety of textures
and styles of the furniture, which is elaborately
juxtaposed with ornaments in space.

Color Matching

The overall color in the space is calm and tranquil with a fundamental tone of palm and gray colors, which symbolize wisdom, calmness, nobility and elegance in nature. Collaborated with innately elegant rose gold color, Hermes symbolically classic orange color and neutral shades, the space achieves infinite balance of proportions, emotions and stories. Primarily, the design takes the post-modernism as the main style, and exhibits powerful space aesthetics via specific function and unique flavor achieved by its colors and furnishings. The mass use of black, white and gray colors makes the space integrated. The tone of palm and gray colors, coupled with khaki and beige colors, clash in small areas with the collaboration of Chinese and Western elements, making the overall space calm, graceful and varied as well.

Hua Ting Mansion No.13

- Magnificent and Changeable Prospect

▶ Modern Luxury
  Style

Designer
Juliet Law (Domus
Design&Engineering
Co., Ltd.)

Photographer
BAO Shiwang

Area
500m²

Materials
silver-black color marble/
stainless veneer/wooden
veneer/de Gournay hand-
painted wall paper/SICIS
mosaic tile/Danilo wall
paint/wrought iron/art floor

Location
Shanghai, China

Led by the Italian designer Juliet Law from Domus Design&Engineering, an impressionist painter, the project is designed in bold color matching, from which the inner world of the designer is lively and expertly exhibited.

Inspired by conceptual elements of Italian top luxuries, the design is novel, unique, modern, magnificent and delicate with good taste, leaving a profound impression. The appropriate application of specular reflection technique doubles the space, giving no repeated or cliche visual effect. The space is humanity-oriented, and specific living space, plus lively colors, is tailored to the needs of each member.

The vertical height reaches 3 meters in the sitting room on the ground floor. The unlocked space between the sitting room and dining hall guarantees the communication among family members. On the first floor, desk as a bridge connects the kid bedroom and the activity area. The second floor is an exclusive area with a huge master bedroom measuring nearly 30m².

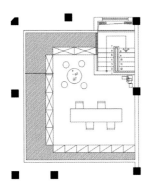

Attic Plan

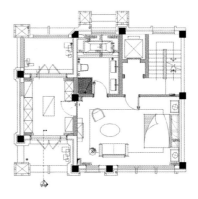

Second floor plan

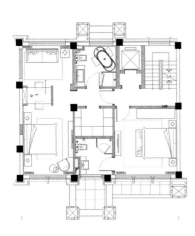

First floor plan

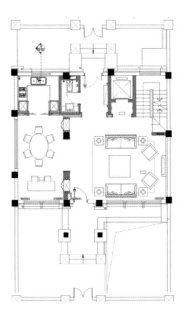

Ground floor plan

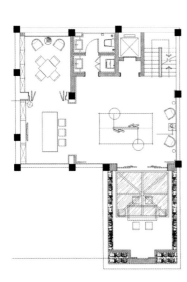

Basement plan

B2 plan

Decoration and Furnishing

In the design of the background wall in the sitting room, de Gournay man-made wallpaper is used, of which vibrant wisteria patterns twine about and extend to chair backs and pillows, creating quiet and comfortable atmosphere.

On the de Gournay man-made wallpaper on the master bedroom ceiling, drawings of cyprinoid, elegant with classic simplicity, convey the idea like "a duck to water" or "treasures fill the home". Collecting memories or looking up at the starlit

sky at the attic is most romantic. The pipelines of solar water heater are tactfully transformed into two "divine inspiring pens", recording every bit of life, and then weaving them into a love letter or a ballad.

Furniture Design and Materials

The flooring is made from black color marbles and SICIS mosaic tiles. The first floor is for the parents. Thus, green color marbles are employed in furniture design and furnishing, and precious marbles are also used on the walls and ground of the bathroom. All of this creates solemn and serene leisure space.

Sunshine is the theme of kid bedroom and the French windows on three sides meet the need of daylight. In addition, lively green color and dynamic element of skateboarding forms an image of fine young men.

The background wall of the master bedroom on the second floor is entirely made of man-made mosaic tiles. The invisible door at the fireplace is a special design for surprise.

In view of the housewife's daily life, the designers created a leisure space on basement 1, including chess & card room, baking area and outdoor courtyard where housewives can exchange card experience, bake cookies and chat over the teatime. This is an elegant and delicate lifestyle typical for modern women.

Basement 2 is exclusive to the male, including cigar area, double-deck wine cabinet, and Hi-Fi audiovisual room. Equipped with velvet sofas in gray and Hermes orange, the lifestyle is upgraded. The use of leather and stainless steel manifests wisdom and attractively rugged aura of businessman. As sports are indispensable to life, the well-equipped fitness area manifests the extraordinary qualities of the successful host—robustness and competitiveness.

INDEX

© 2017 by Design Media Publishing (UK) Limited
Published in December 2017

Design Media Publishing (UK) Limited
Chase Business Centre
39-41 Chase Side
London
N14 5BP
Tel/Fax: +44(0)20 3182 0016
www.designmediauk.com
Email: info@designmediauk.com

This is translation of *Interior and Decoration of Villa*,
the edition first published 2017
©2017 by Liaoning Science and Technology Publishing
House Ltd.
ISBN: 978-7-5591-0304-8
By Yu Fang

ISBN 978-1-912268-29-0

Editing: Ariel Yu
Translation: Sun Zhe
Proofreading: Katy Lee
Design/Layout: Guan Muzi

Printed in China